SCHOLASTIC

Perfect Poems

With Strategies for Building Fluency

GRADES 3–4

Good night!

NEW YORK • TORONTO • LONDON • AUCKLAND • SYDNEY
MEXICO CITY • NEW DELHI • HONG KONG • BUENOS AIRES

Teaching *Resources*

ACKNOWLEDGMENTS

Every effort has been made to contact copyright holders for permission to reproduce borrowed material. The publisher regrets any oversights that may have occurred and will be pleased to rectify them in subsequent reprints of the work.

The material on pages 4–13 has been adapted from BUILDING FLUENCY: LESSONS AND STRATEGIES FOR READING SUCCESS by Wiley Blevins (Scholastic, 2001). Adapted and reprinted by permission of the publisher.

"Opposites" copyright © 2000 by Linda Ross. Used by permission of the author.

"Squirrel and Acorn" by Beverly McLoughland first appeared in *Spider* Magazine, June 1998. Reprinted by permission of the author who controls all rights.

"Think of It" by Bette Killion. Copyright © 1990 by Scholastic Inc. Used by permission of the publisher.

"Curious Questions" copyright © 1973 by Bobbi Katz. Used by permission of the author.

"Color My Mood" copyright © 1999 by Mary Sullivan. Used by permission of the author.

"I'm Not Scared!" by Karen Baicker. Copyright © by Scholastic Inc. Used by permission of the publisher.

"Planet Roll Call" from 101 SCIENCE POEMS AND SONGS FOR YOUNG LEARNERS by Meish Goldish. Copyright © 1996 by Meish Goldish. Reprinted by permission of the author.

"A Trip to the Store" by Pamela Chanko. Copyright © by Scholastic Inc. Used by permission of the publisher.

"What Do You Say to a Bug?" copyright © 2000 by Cynthia Pederson. Used by permission of Marian Reiner for the author.

"Chocolate Cake" from ALL THE DAY LONG by Nina Payne. Copyright © 1973 by Nina Payne. Reprinted by permission of the author.

"More Disgusting Broccoli Pie, Please!" by Karen Baicker. Copyright © by Scholastic Inc. Used by permission of the publisher.

"The Bremen Town Musicians" from ONCE UPON A TIME IN RHYME: 28 FOLK AND FAIRY TALE POEMS AND SONGS by Meish Goldish. Copyright © 1995 by Scholastic Inc. Used by permission of the publisher.

"Could We Be Friends?" by Bobbi Katz. Copyright © 1972 by Encyclopedia Britannica. Copyright © 1992 by Bobbi Katz. Used by permission of the author.

"Let Me Dream of Peanut Butter" copyright © 1999 by Mary Sullivan. Used by permission of the author.

"If Dogs Could Talk" from PLAYFUL POEMS THAT BUILD READING SKILLS copyright © 2000 by Kirk Mann. Reprinted by permission of Scholastic Inc.

"Colors and Questions" copyright © 1982 by Bobbi Katz. Reprinted by permission of the author.

"How Barney Lost His Snore" by Helen O'Reilly from 70 WONDERFUL WORD FAMILY POEMS. Used by permission of Scholastic Inc.

"Flu" by Terry Cooper. Copyright © by Scholastic Inc. Used by permission of the publisher.

"Maps" by Carol Weston. Copyright © by Scholastic Inc. Used by permission of the publisher.

"Bubble Gum" from ALL THE DAY LONG by Nina Payne. Copyright © 1973 by Nina Payne. Reprinted by permission of the author.

"City Spring" by Beverly McLoughland first appeared in *Cricket* Magazine, May 1990. Reprinted by permission of the author who controls all rights.

"I speak, I say, I talk" by Arnold L. Shapiro. Copyright © 1963 by World Book, Inc. from ONCE UPON A TIME, Volume 1 of Childcraft.

"Laughing Time" by William Jay Smith. From LAUGHING TIME by William Jay Smith. Copyright © 1953, 1955 by William Jay Smith. Reprinted by permission of Farrar, Straus and Giroux.

"The City Mouse and the Country Mouse" from ONCE UPON A TIME IN RHYME: 28 FOLK AND FAIRY TALE POEMS AND SONGS by Meish Goldish. Copyright © 1995 by Scholastic Inc. Used by permission of the publisher.

"Tip-Toe Tale" by Dixie Wilson from *Child Life* Magazine.

"Rice Pudding" by A.A. Milne from WHEN WE WERE VERY YOUNG. Copyright © 1924 by E.P. Dutton, renewed 1952 by A.A. Milne.

"The Princess and the Pea" from ONCE UPON A TIME IN RHYME: 28 FOLK AND FAIRY TALE POEMS AND SONGS by Meish Goldish. Copyright © 1995 by Scholastic Inc. Used by permission of the publisher.

"Valentine's Day" from THEMATIC POEMS, SONGS, AND FINGERPLAYS by Meish Goldish. Copyright © 1993 by Scholastic Inc. Used by permission of the publisher.

"The Land of Imagination" copyright © 1997 by Helen H. Moore. Used by permission of the author.

"A Mortifying Mistake" by Anna M. Pratt. From HUMOROUS POETRY FOR CHILDREN edited by William Cole.

"Shy" from FATHERS, MOTHERS, SISTERS, BROTHERS by Mary Ann Hoberman. Copyright © 1991 by Mary Ann Hoberman. By permission of Little, Brown and Company.

"Spaghetti! Spaghetti!" from RAINY, RAINY SATURDAY by Jack Prelutsky. Copyright © 1980 by Jack Prelutsky. Used by permission of HarperCollins Publishers.

"The World of Animals" from 101 SCIENCE POEMS AND SONGS FOR YOUNG LEARNERS by Meish Goldish. Copyright © 1996 by Meish Goldish. Reprinted by permission of the author and Scholastic Inc.

"The Sad, Sad Story of the Piggy Who Got None" copyright © 1997 by Helen H. Moore. Used by permission of the author.

Cover design by Maria Lilja
Interior illustrations by Kate Flanagan, Brian Floca, Mike Gordon,
Mark A. Hicks, Mike Moran, and Bari Weissman
Interior design by Holly Grundon

ISBN 0-439-43831-4

Contents

What Is Reading Fluency?

Fluency: A Definition

Listening to children read—whether it's a piece of their own writing or an excerpt from a favorite trade book can tell us a lot about their reading progress. An oral reading that is smooth, accurate, and that uses the correct intonation and phrasing reflects a reader who understands the text and has mastered basic decoding skills. An oral reading that is slow, labored, and lacking in expression is characteristic of a child who lacks reading proficiency or is reading a text beyond his or her reading level. Therefore, a child's reading fluency is one important measure of a child's reading progress.

According to A *Dictionary of Reading and Related Terms* (Harris and Hodges, 1981), fluency is "the ability to read smoothly, easily, and readily with freedom from word-recognition problems." Fluency is necessary for good comprehension and enjoyable reading (Nathan and Stanovich, 1991). A lack of fluency is characterized by a slow, halting pace; frequent mistakes; poor phrasing; and inadequate intonation (Samuels, 1979)—all the result of weak word-recognition skills.

Fluent reading is a major goal of reading instruction because decoding print accurately and effortlessly enables students to read for meaning. According to Chall's Stages of Reading Development, fluency begins around grades 2 to 3 for many students. During this fluency stage, the reader becomes "unglued" from the print; that is, students can recognize many words quickly and accurately by sight and are skilled at sounding out those they don't recognize. For some students, however, fluency requires additional instruction and guided practice in foundational skills throughout the elementary years. Basically, a fluent reader can:

1. **read at a rapid rate (pace—the speed at which oral or silent reading occurs).**

2. **automatically recognize words (smoothness/accuracy—efficient decoding skills).**

3. **phrase correctly (prosody—the ability to read a text orally using appropriate pitch, stress, and phrasing).**

Nonfluent readers read slowly and spend so much time trying to identify unfamiliar words that they have trouble comprehending what they're reading.

Automaticity theory, developed by LaBerge and Samuels (1974) helps explain how reading fluency develops. Automaticity refers to knowing how to do something so well you don't have to think about it. As tasks become easier, they require less attention and practice. Think of a child learning to play basketball. As initial attention is focused on how to dribble the ball, it's difficult for the child to think about guarding the ball from opponents, shooting a basket, or even running quickly down the court. However, over time, lots of practice makes dribbling almost second nature. The player is ready to concentrate on higher-level aspects of the game.

For reading, automaticity refers to the ability to accurately and quickly recognize many words as whole units. The advantage of recognizing a word as a whole unit is that words have meaning, and less memory is required for a meaningful word than for a meaningless letter. The average child needs between 4 and 14 exposures to a new word to recognize it automatically. However, children with reading difficulties need 40 or more exposures to a new word. Therefore, it's critical that students get a great deal of practice reading texts at their independent reading level to develop automaticity (Beck & Juel, 1995; Samuels, Schermer & Reinking, 1992).

To commit words to memory, children need to decode many words sound by sound, and then progress to recognizing the larger word chunks. Then, instead of focusing on sounding out words sound by sound, the reader can read whole words, thereby focusing attention on decoding and comprehension simultaneously. In fact, the hallmark of fluent reading is the ability to decode and comprehend at the same time.

Although research has shown that fluency is a critical factor in reading development, many teachers and publishers have failed to recognize its importance to overall reading proficiency. Few teachers teach fluency directly, and elementary reading textbooks give fluency instruction short shrift. Consequently, Allington (1983) has called fluency the "neglected goal" of reading instruction.

There are many reasons why children fail to read fluently. They include the following (Allington, 1983; Blevins, 2002):

Lack of foundational skills

Some children have not mastered basic decoding skills or sight word recognition of the most frequent words in text. Therefore, when they are confronted with more complex text containing longer sentences and more multisyllabic words, their reading breaks down.

Lack of practice time

Good readers generally spend more time reading during instructional time and therefore become better readers. Good readers also engage in more silent reading. This additional practice stimulates their reading growth. Poor readers spend less time actually reading.

Frustration

Good readers are exposed to more text at their independent reading level, whereas poor readers frequently encounter text at their frustration level. Consequently poor readers tend to give up because they make so many errors.

Lack of exposure

Some children have never been exposed to fluent reading models. These children come from homes in which there are few books and little or no reading.

Missing the "why" of reading

Good readers tend to view reading as making meaning from text, whereas poor readers tend to view reading as trying to read words accurately.

The good-reader syndrome

In school, good readers are more likely to get positive feedback and more likely to be encouraged to read with expression and make meaning from text. Poor readers receive less positive feedback and the focus of their instruction is often solely on figuring out words or attending to word parts.

How to Develop Fluency

Although few reading-textbook teacher manuals contain instruction on building fluency, there are in fact many things you can do to develop your students' fluency. Rasinski (1989) has identified six key ways to build fluency.

1. Model fluent reading

Students need many opportunities to hear texts read. This can include daily teacher read alouds, books on tape, poems, and texts read by peers during sharing time. It's particularly critical for poorer readers who've been placed in a low reading group to hear text read correctly because they are likely to repeatedly hear the efforts of other poor readers in their group. They need proficient, fluent models; that is, they need to have a model voice in their heads to refer to as they monitor their own reading. While you read aloud to students, periodically highlight aspects of fluent reading. For example, point out how you read dialogue the way you think the character might have said it or how you speed up your reading when the text becomes more intense and exciting. Talk about fluency—how to achieve it, and why it's important. Constantly remind students that with practice they can become fluent readers. An important benefit of daily read alouds is that they expose students to a wider range of vocabulary.

2. Provide direct instruction and feedback

Direct instruction and feedback in fluency includes, but isn't limited to, independent reading practice, fluent reading modeling, and monitoring students' reading rates. Here are some ways to include lots of this needed instruction in your classroom.

* Explicitly teach students sound-spelling correspondences they struggle with, high-utility decoding and syllabication strategies, and a large core of sight words.

* Occasionally time students' reading. Have students create charts to monitor their own progress. Encourage them to set new reading-rate goals.

* Find alternatives to round-robin reading. Round-robin reading is one of the most harmful techniques for developing fluency. During round-robin reading, students read aloud only a small portion of the text. Although they are supposed to be following along with the

other readers, often they don't. It is absolutely essential that students read a lot every day. When they're reading a new story or poem, it is important that they read the entire text—often more than once. One way to avoid round-robin reading is to have students read the text silently a few pages at a time and then ask them questions or have them comment on strategies they used. Other appropriate techniques include partner reading, reading softly to themselves while you circulate and "listen in," and popcorn reading, in which students are called on frequently and randomly (often in the middle of a paragraph or stanza) to read aloud. If you use any technique in which students have not read the entire text during their reading group, be sure that they read it in its entirety before or after the reading group.

❁ Teach appropriate phrasing and intonation. Guided oral reading practice and the study of punctuation and grammar can help. For teaching phrasing, see phrase-cued text practice on page 11. For teaching intonation and punctuation, use some or all of the following. Have students:

◆ recite the alphabet as a conversation.
ABCD? EFG! HI? JKL. MN? OPQ. RST! UVWX. YZ!

◆ recite the same sentence using different punctuation.
Cows moo. Cows moo? Cows moo!

◆ practice placing the stress on different words in the same sentence.
I am happy. I _am_ happy. I am <u>happy</u>.

◆ practice reading sentences as if talking to a friend.

Studying grammar fosters fluency because grammar alerts the reader to natural phrases in a sentence. For example, being able to identify the subject and the predicate of a sentence is one step in understanding phrase boundaries in text. Also, understanding the role of prepositions and conjunctions adds additional clues to phrase boundaries. Try providing students with short passages color-coded according to subject and predicate to assist them in practice reading.

❁ Conduct 2-minute drills to underline or locate a target word, syllable, or spelling pattern in an array or short passage (Moats, 1998). This will help students rapidly recognize spelling patterns that are common to many words. And it's a lot of fun.

3. Provide reader support (choral reading and reading-while-listening)

Readers need to practice reading both orally and silently. Research has shown that oral reading is very important for the developing reader, especially younger children. It appears that young children need to hear themselves read, and they benefit from adult feedback. As well as improving reading, this feedback shows students how highly we adults value the skill of reading. There are several ways to support students' oral reading without evoking the fear and humiliation struggling readers often feel when called on to read aloud. Here are the most popular techniques (always use text at the student's instructional level that models natural language patterns).

- Reading simultaneously with a partner or small group. With this technique, students can "float" in and out as appropriate without feeling singled out. For best results, have students practice reading the selection independently before reading it with the partner or group.

- Echo reading. As you read a phrase or sentence in the text, the student repeats it. This continues throughout the text. You can also use a tape recording of the text with pauses for the child to echo the reading.

- Choral reading. Reading together as a group is great for poetry and selections with a distinct pattern. Students are challenged to read at the same pace and with the same phrasing and intonation as the rest of the group.

- Paired repeated readings (Koskinen and Blum, 1986). A student reads a short text three times to a partner and gets feedback. Then the partners switch roles. To avoid frustration, it works best to pair above-level readers with on-level readers and on-level readers with below-level readers.

- Books and poems on tape. Select and place appropriate books and poems on tape in a classroom Listening Center. Have students follow along as the text is read, reading with the narrator where possible.

4. Repeated readings of one text

Repeated reading, a popular technique developed by Samuels (1979), has long been recognized as an excellent way to help students achieve fluency. It has been shown to increase reading rate and accuracy and to transfer to new texts. As a child reads a passage at his or her instructional level, the teacher times the reading. The teacher then gives feedback on word-recognition errors and the number of words per minute the child read accurately, and records this data on a graph. (To use poetry for repeated readings in grades 3–4, the poem should contain about 125 words.) The child then practices reading the same selection independently or with a partner. The process is repeated and the child's progress plotted on the graph until the child masters the text. This charting is effective because (1) students become focused on their own mastery of the task and competing with their own past performance, and (2) students have concrete evidence that they are making progress. In addition, repeating the words many times helps students build a large sight-word vocabulary.

Students who resist rereading selections need incentives. Besides simply telling the student that rereading is a part of the important practice one does to become a better reader, you might motivate her by having her:

- ◆ read to a friend, family member, or pet,
- ◆ read to a student in a lower grade,
- ◆ read into a tape player to record the session,
- ◆ set a reading-rate goal for a given piece of text and try to exceed that goal in successive readings.

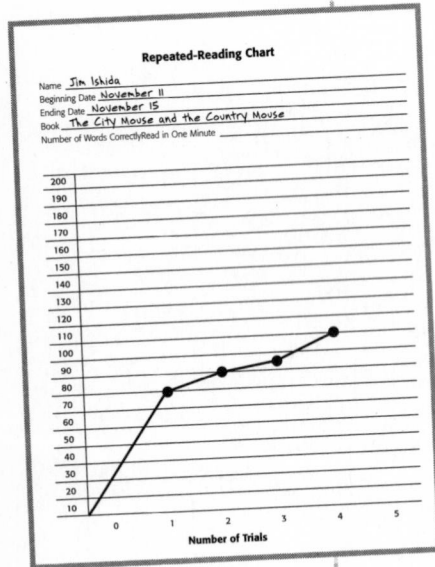

Repeated-Reading Chart

Name _Jim Ishida_
Beginning Date _November 11_
Ending Date _November 15_
Book _The City Mouse and the Country Mouse_
Number of Words Correctly Read in One Minute _____

Number of Trials

5. Cueing phrase boundaries in text

One of the characteristics of proficient (fluent) readers is the ability to group words together in meaningful units—syntactically appropriate phrases. "Proficient reading is characterized not only by fast and accurate word recognition, but also by readers' word chunking or phrasing behavior while reading connected discourse." (Rasinski, 1989) Students who are having trouble with comprehension may not be putting words together in meaningful phrases or chunks as they read. Their oral reading is characterized by a choppy, word-by-word delivery that impedes comprehension. These students need instruction in phrasing written text into appropriate segments.

One way to help students learn to recognize and use natural English phrase boundaries—and thus improve their phrasing, fluency, and comprehension—is phrase-cued text practice. Phrase-cued text is a short passage marked by a slash (or some other visual) at the end of each phrase break. The longer pause at the end of the sentence is marked by a double slash (//). The teacher models good oral reading, and students practice with the marked text. Later, students apply their skills to the same text, unmarked. Have students practice the skill orally for 10 minutes daily.

Here's an example:

In the summer/I like/to swim/at the beach.//

Although it's very hot/I like the idea/

of being in the cool water

all day.// Summer truly is/

my favorite time/of the year.//

6. Providing students with easy reading materials

Students need an enormous amount of individualized reading practice in decodable materials that are not too difficult (Beck & Juel, 1995; Samuels, Schermer & Reinking, 1992). Aim for at least 30 minutes of independent reading every day. Some should occur in school, and some can occur at home. Fluency develops through a great deal of practice reading texts in which students can use sound-spelling strategies (as opposed to contextual strategies) to figure out a majority of the unfamiliar words. In the early grades, there must be a match between instruction in phonics and reading practice—hence the need for practice stories and poems that are decodable (Blevins, 2002). This match encourages students to adopt sound-spelling strategies and at the same time, through extensive practice reading text after text after text, leads to fluent reading. It is critical that practice reading materials be at a child's independent or instructional reading level, *not* at the child's frustration level. In other words, the student's reading accuracy (the proportion of words read correctly) should be above 90 percent. During individualized practice, students may be reading at different levels. They read aloud "quietly" to themselves as the teacher walks around listening to each child for a minute or so while still monitoring the group as a whole. Students need time to figure out unfamiliar words through phonics patterns. Expecting students to read fluently when they are not fluent only encourages guessing and memorization.

Using Poetry to Build Fluency

Poetry lends itself beautifully to fluency instruction and practice. The length and natural rhythms of most poems give them a musical quality that's enjoyable to listen to and perform. Poetry often contains a wide range of punctuation and phrasing, two key aspects of fluency. In addition, poems are fun ways to practice one's decoding skills.

The poems in this collection are divided into four categories:

1. **Poems for Partners and Small Groups**

   These poems are ideal for students to read together. Some contain multiple parts perfect for Reader's Theater; others have repetitive stanzas that are fun for choral reading. Working together gives students an opportunity to provide peers with constructive feedback, thereby verbalizing their understanding of fluent reading.

2. **Poems to Build Intonation and Phrasing**

   These poems focus on varying the pace and expression of oral readings. The variety of sentence types and phrase boundaries helps students to pay attention to these important aspects of reading. In addition, the chunking of text into meaningful units, line by line, is one way to introduce or reinforce aspects of grammar useful in reading fluently (subject, predicate, prepositional phrases).

3. **Poems to Build Recognition of Phonics Patterns and Sight Words**

   These poems focus on one or two key phonics patterns common to early reading materials. The repetition of the patterns helps students to easily recognize these larger word chunks so useful in decoding longer words.

4. **Poems for Repeated Readings**

   These poems are more complex and comprehensive. They require students to pull together all aspects of fluent reading and encourage students to practice enough so that a formal, dramatic reading is the ultimate result.

Instructional Routine

Use the following routine for introducing each poem.

STEP 1: Distribute copies of the poem or write the poem on chart paper. As an alternative, make a transparency of the poem and show it on the overhead projector.

STEP 2: Read aloud the poem. Highlight one or two aspects of fluency, such as intonation or phrasing. Discuss these aspects of fluency and model them using selected sentences or phrases from the poem.

STEP 3: Do an echo reading of the poem. Read aloud each stanza and have students repeat using the same pace, accuracy, and expression.

STEP 4: Assign the poem to partners, small groups, or individuals based on the goal of each poem. For example, poems designed for repeated readings should be assigned to individuals, whereas poems for choral readings should be assigned to small groups.

STEP 5: Provide time throughout the week for students to practice reading aloud their poems. Circulate and listen in. Provide feedback on key aspects of fluent reading. Then, allow students to share their readings at the end of the week.

Above all, have fun with the poems in this book. Poems are like language amusement parks; they represent the works of those playing with language in rhythmic and creative ways. Sharing the joys of written language with students is a wonderful and valuable gift.

Opposites

BY LINDA B. ROSS

Do you know about opposites?
Let's see if you do!
What's the opposite of many?
The opposite is few.

What's the opposite of bottom?
The opposite is top.
And what's the opposite of go?
The opposite is stop.

What's the opposite of cold?
The opposite is hot.
And what's the opposite of a little?
The opposite is a lot.

Here is the last pair of opposites.
Get ready, it's going to be hard!
What's the opposite of even?
The opposite is odd.

Perfect Poems With Strategies for Building Fluency: Grades 3–4   Scholastic Teaching Resources

Fire! Fire!

—TRADITIONAL

"Fire! Fire!"
Cried Mrs. McGuire.
"Where? Where?"
Cried Mrs. Blair.
"All over town!"
Cried Mrs. Brown.
"Get some water!"
Cried her daughter.
"We'd better jump!"
Cried Mrs. Gump.
"That would be silly!"
Cried Mrs. Minelli.
"It looks too risky!"
Cried Mrs. Matruski.
"What'll we do?"
Cried Mrs. LaRue.
"Turn in the alarm!"
Cried Mrs. Starm.
"Save us! Save us!"
Cried Mrs. Davis.

The fire department got the call
And the firemen saved them one and all.

Squirrel and Acorn

BY BEVERLY MCLOUGHLAND

Where's that nut
I hid in the fall?
Bad news!
Bad news!
Can't recall.
Must think,
Try hard,
Somewhere
In the yard.
Look here,
Look there,
Bad news!
Nowhere!

I'm here
Below,
Just under the
Snow,
Off to his
Right—
Well out of
Sight.
He can't
Recall?
Then I'll
Grow tall.
Could be a
Tree.
Good news!
Good news!
Good news
For me!

Perfect Poems With Strategies for Building Fluency: Grades 3–4   Scholastic Teaching Resources

Curious Questions

BY BOBBI KATZ

Have you ever seen a fish that walked?
Have you ever heard a grasshopper talk?
If you ask me how I know that they do,
I'll hop on one foot and say
Doodle-dee-doo!

Have you ever seen a tomcat reading a book?
Do you know a walrus who skates on a brook?
If you ask me how I know that they do,
I'll hop on one foot and say
Doodle-dee-doo!

Have you ever seen a hippo who danced on her toes?
Did you meet a horse in a store buying clothes?
If you ask me how I know that they do,
I'll hop on one foot and say
Doodle-dee-doo!

Have you ever seen a fox blow a jazz clarinet?
Have you ever heard a duck quacking, "Don't get me wet!"
If you ask me how I know that they do,
I'll hop on one foot and say
Doodle-dee-doo!

Color My Mood

BY MARY SULLIVAN

Colors name the way we feel.
When we're angry or we're sad:

I'm blue when I'm lonely,
I'm red when I'm mad.

I'm green when I'm jealous,
I'm pink when I'm glad.

I'm orange when I'm good,
I'm purple when I'm bad.

And I made up a new name
For when I'm feeling mellow.

I think I'm gonna call it:
Lemon Jell-o yellow!

Perfect Poems With Strategies for Building Fluency: Grades 3–4   Scholastic Teaching Resources

Think of It

BY BETTE KILLION

"Go quickly," says my mother
or some other
hurry person.
　Then I think of fast things—
　　hummingbird wings
　　lizards darting
　　racers starting
　　bicycle wheels
　　automobiles
　　wind through the trees
　　some angry bees—
and I'm quick!

Continued

"Sh-h-h!" says my mother
or some other
tiptoe person.
   Then I think of still things—
      empty swings
      dark nights
      soaring kites
      thick, soft mittens
      newborn kittens
      whispered prayers
      sleeping bears—
and I'm quiet!

"Slow down," says my mother
or some other
getting-tired person.
   Then I think of lazy things—
      yawning kings
      elephants strolling
      plump pigs rolling
      a cow chewing cud
      some oozing mud
      inchworm on my hand
      sifting sand—
and I go slow!

I'm Not Scared!

BY KAREN BAICKER

Reader 1:
I'm not afraid of anything,
Not anything at all,
Not wriggling snakes or spiders
Who are climbing up my wall.

Reader 2:
Well, my friend, if you must know
I'm not as brave as that.
I'm afraid of my own shadow,
A great big scaredy-cat.

Reader 1:
You know that you can stick with me
When your stomach's in a knot.
I'll hold your hand and show you
All the courage that you've got.

Reader 2:
Already I am feeling braver,
Just by knowing you.
I'm not afraid, but what's that noise?
Don't you hear it?

Boo!

Ladies and Jelly Spoons

—ANONYMOUS

Ladies and jelly spoons:
I come before you
To stand behind you
And tell you something
I know nothing about.

Next Thursday,
The day after Friday,
There'll be a ladies' meeting
For men only.

Wear your best clothes
If you haven't any,
And if you can come
Please stay home.

Admission is free,
You can pay at the door.
We'll give you a seat
So you can sit on the floor.

It makes no difference
Where you sit;
The kid in the gallery
Is sure to spit.

Perfect Poems With Strategies for Building Fluency: Grades 3–4   Scholastic Teaching Resources

Fooba Wooba John

—TRADITIONAL

Saw a snail chase a whale,
Fooba Wooba, Fooba Wooba,
Saw a snail chase a whale,
Fooba Wooba John.

Saw a snail chase a whale,
All around the water pail.
Hey, John, ho, John,
Fooba Wooba John.

Saw a frog chase a dog,
Fooba Wooba, Fooba Wooba,
Saw a frog chase a dog,
Fooba Wooba John.

Saw a frog chase a dog,
Sitting on a hollow log.
Hey, John, ho, John,
Fooba Wooba John.

Saw a flea kick a tree,
Fooba Wooba, Fooba Wooba,
Saw a flea kick a tree,
Fooba Wooba John.

Saw a flea kick a tree,
In the middle of the sea.
Hey, John, ho, John,
Fooba Wooba John.

Heard a cow say meow,
Fooba Wooba, Fooba Wooba,
Heard a cow say meow,
Fooba Wooba John.

Heard a cow say meow,
Then I heard it say bow-wow.
Hey, John, ho, John,
Fooba Wooba John.

Planet Roll Call

BY MEISH GOLDISH

Nine planets around the sun,
Listen as I call each one:

Mercury? Here! Number one,
Closest planet to the sun.

Venus? Here! Number two,
Shining bright, just like new!

Earth? Here! Number three,
Earth is home to you and me.

Mars? Here! Number four,
Red and ready to explore!

Jupiter? Here! Number five,
Largest planet, that's no jive!

Saturn? Here! Number six,
With rings of dust and ice that mix.

Uranus? Here! Number seven,
A planet tilted high in heaven.

Neptune? Here! Number eight,
With one dark spot whose size is great.

Pluto? Here! Number nine,
The smallest and the last in line!

*Perfect Poems With Strategies
for Building Fluency: Grades 3–4*
Scholastic Teaching Resources

Limericks

—ANONYMOUS

I raised a great hullabaloo
When I found a large mouse in my stew.
    Said the waiter, "Don't shout
    and wave it about,
Or the rest will be wanting one, too!"

There was an old man of Peru
Who dreamed he was eating his shoe.
    He woke in the night
    In a terrible fright,
And found it was perfectly true.

A Trip to the Store

BY PAMELA CHANKO

Reader 1:
One day we had to go to the store,
Which really is not our favorite chore.
Dad needed a mop to clean up the floor.
Mom needed milk and a whole lot more.
A trip to the store is a terrible bore.
Then all of a sudden we heard a great roar!

Reader 2:
We'd never heard anything like it before.
So we turned, and we saw . . . a big dinosaur!
We asked him what he was looking for,
And he asked us to show him the way to the store.
So we bought milk and a mop and a whole lot more,
And learned something we never knew before.

Together:
A trip to the store is never a bore—
As long as you go with a big dinosaur!

Perfect Poems With Strategies for Building Fluency: Grades 3–4   Scholastic Teaching Resources

I Know an Old Lady Who Swallowed a Fly

—TRADITIONAL

I know an old lady who swallowed a fly.
I don't know why she swallowed the fly.
Perhaps she'll die.

I know an old lady who swallowed a spider
That wiggled and jiggled and tickled inside her.
She swallowed the spider to catch a fly,
But I don't know why she swallowed the fly.
Perhaps she'll die.

I know an old lady who swallowed a bird.
How absurd to swallow a bird!
She swallowed the bird to catch a spider
That wiggled and jiggled and tickled inside her.
She swallowed the spider to catch a fly,
But I don't know why she swallowed the fly.
Perhaps she'll die.

I know an old lady who swallowed a cat.
Think of that, she swallowed a cat!
She swallowed the cat to catch a bird.
She swallowed the bird to catch a spider
That wiggled and jiggled and tickled inside her.
She swallowed the spider to catch a fly,
But I don't know why she swallowed the fly.
Perhaps she'll die.

Continued

I know an old lady who swallowed a dog.
Oh, what a hog to swallow a dog!
She swallowed the dog to catch a cat,
She swallowed the cat to catch a bird.
She swallowed the bird to catch a spider
That wiggled and jiggled and tickled inside her.
She swallowed the spider to catch a fly,
But I don't know why she swallowed the fly.
Perhaps she'll die.

I know an old lady who swallowed a goat.
Popped open her throat and swallowed a goat!
She swallowed the goat to catch a dog.
She swallowed the dog to catch a cat,
She swallowed the cat to catch a bird.
She swallowed the bird to catch a spider
That wiggled and jiggled and tickled inside her.
She swallowed the spider to catch a fly,
But I don't know why she swallowed the fly.
Perhaps she'll die.

I know an old lady who swallowed a cow.
Don't ask how she swallowed a cow.
She swallowed the cow to catch a goat.
She swallowed the goat to catch a dog.
She swallowed the dog to catch a cat,
She swallowed the cat to catch a bird.
She swallowed the bird to catch a spider
That wiggled and jiggled and tickled inside her.
She swallowed the spider to catch a fly,
But I don't know why she swallowed the fly.
Perhaps she'll die.

I know an old lady who swallowed a horse.
She died, of course!

Perfect Poems With Strategies for Building Fluency: Grades 3–4   Scholastic Teaching Resources

Penny Problem

BY MAXWELL HIGGINS

Abe Lincoln was a BIG man—
A GIANT in every way—
With GREAT LONG LEGS
And a GREAT TALL HAT
And a GREAT BIG HEART, they say.

And he dreamed BIG DREAMS for our country:
That one day, all people would be FREE,
That we'd be one STRONG, UNITED nation,
That we'd live in PEACE and HARMONY.

But when I look at Abe Lincoln on a penny
A leader who in history stands TALL,
I wonder just how it is they managed
To fit him on a coin

so

small.

What Do You Say to a Bug?

BY CYNTHIA PEDERSON

Some say *Ugly*!
Some just *Ugh*!
when they see
most any bug.
But I say, "Yeah!
Let grass-hop, ant-dance, beetle-bop, roly-poly play."

Some say *Ugly*!
Some just *Ugh*!
What do <u>you</u> say
to a bug?

Perfect Poems With Strategies for Building Fluency: Grades 3–4   Scholastic Teaching Resources

Chocolate Cake

BY NINA PAYNE

Chocolate cake
chocolate cake
that's the one
I'll help you make
Flour soda
salt are sifted
butter sugar
cocoa lifted
by the eggs
then mix the whole
grease the pans
I'll lick the bowl
Chocolate caked
chocolate caked
that's what I'll be
when it's baked.

If You Ever

—TRADITIONAL

If you ever ever ever ever ever
  If you ever ever ever meet a whale
You must never never never never never
  You must never never never touch his tail.

For if you ever ever ever ever ever
  If you ever ever ever touch his tail,
You will never never never never never
  You will never never never meet another whale.

Perfect Poems With Strategies for Building Fluency: Grades 3–4 Scholastic Teaching Resources

More Disgusting Broccoli Pie, Please!

BY KAREN BAICKER

"It's dinner time," my mama said,
"So please come and sit down.
I made a special dish just for
Your grandma who's in town."
I took one look and held my nose
And said, "I'd rather die
Than take one tiny bite of that
Disgusting broccoli pie."
"It's not so bad," she said to me.
"Don't act like it's a chore.
You'll eat or else you'll go upstairs
And shut your bedroom door."
"Oh poor me!" I moaned and cried,
"It isn't any use!"
I took a breath and took a bite
And washed it down with juice.
I closed my eyes and swallowed fast
Then gave a mighty roar,
"Don't just sit there, can't you see
I NEED A LITTLE MORE!"

Annie Mae

—TRADITIONAL

Annie Mae, where are you going?
Up the stairs to take a bath.
Annie Mae with legs like toothpicks
And a neck like a giraffe.
Annie Mae stepped in the bathtub.
Annie Mae pulled out the plug.
Oh my goodness!
Oh my soul!
There goes Annie Mae down that hole.
Annie Mae?
Annie Mae?
Gurgle, gurgle, glug.

Perfect Poems With Strategies for Building Fluency: Grades 3–4   Scholastic Teaching Resources

The Washing Machine

BY JEFFREY DAVIES

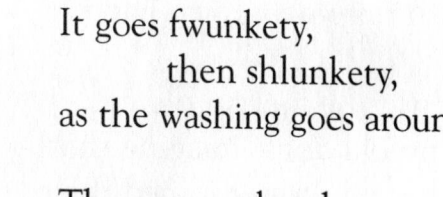

It goes fwunkety,
      then shlunkety,
as the washing goes around.

The water spluncheses
      and it schluncheses,
as the washing goes around.

As you pick it out it splocheses,
      then it flocheses,
as the washing goes around.

But at the end it schlopperies,
      and it flopperies,
and the washing stops going round.

The Bremen Town Musicians

BY MEISH GOLDISH

There was a donkey old and slow.
Off to Bremen he decided to go.
He said, "My voice is still quite grand.
I will sing with the Bremen Town band!"

Sing, sing, sing,
Sing with the Bremen Town band!

Along the way, he met an old cat,
And then an old dog—imagine that!
And then an old rooster joined them, too.
They all agreed on what they'd do:

Sing, sing, sing,
Sing with the Bremen Town band!

"Hee-haw!" "Meow, meow!"
They sang as loud as they knew how!
"Arf-arf!" "Cock-a-doodle-doo!"
The thieves got scared and off they flew!

The donkey, the rooster, dog, and cat
Were all so proud—imagine that!
So on the farm they agreed to stay.
Guess what they never did that day?

Sing, sing, sing,
Sing with the Bremen Town band!

Could We Be Friends?

BY BOBBI KATZ

I wonder what your name is.
I wonder who you are—
Kid making faces
          from the back seat
               of a car.
When you stick your tongue out,

               I stick mine out, too.

When you smile and wave to me,

               I wave back at you!

I wonder where your house is—
What games you like to play.
But when the traffic light turns green,

               my father drives away.

Let Me Dream of Peanut Butter

BY MARY SULLIVAN

In my bed, I'm known to mutter,
"Let me dream of peanut butter."

Peanut butter with gobs of jelly.
Peanut butter inside my belly.

Peanut butter on toast with jam
Peanut butter with pickles and ham.

Wait a minute—that's not right. . . .
Wake me up before I bite!

Perfect Poems With Strategies for Building Fluency: Grades 3–4   Scholastic Teaching Resources

In a Dark, Dark Wood

—TRADITIONAL

In a dark, dark wood
There was a dark, dark house,
And in that dark, dark house
There was a dark, dark room,
And in that dark, dark room
There was a dark, dark cupboard,
And in that dark, dark cupboard
There was a dark, dark shelf,
And in that dark, dark shelf
There was a dark, dark box,
And in that dark, dark box
There was a GHOST!

Way Down South

—TRADITIONAL

Way down south
Where bananas grow,
A grasshopper stepped
On an elephant's toe.
The elephant cried
With tears in his eyes,
"Pick on somebody
Your own size!"

Perfect Poems With Strategies for Building Fluency: Grades 3–4 Scholastic Teaching Resources

Thumping, **Stumping,** Bumping, Jumping

—ANONYMOUS

Thumping, stumping, bumping, jumping,
Ripping, nipping, tripping, skipping,
All the way home.

Popping, clopping, stopping, hopping,
Stalking, chalking, talking, walking,
All the way home.

Hillary Hume

—TRADITIONAL

Hillary Hume has a hundred hamsters.
A hundred hamsters has Hillary Hume.
If Hillary Hume has a hundred hamsters,
Will you share a room with Hillary Hume?

Perfect Poems With Strategies for Building Fluency: Grades 3–4   Scholastic Teaching Resources

If Dogs Could Talk

BY KIRK MANN

If dogs could talk I think our dog
Would have a lot to say.
He'd probably tell my little brother,
"SIT and now just STAY."

He'd probably tell my sister,
"How about an ice-cream cone?"
He'd probably tell my mother,
"Please go get me a big bone."

He'd probably tell my father,
"Make a left turn up ahead."
He'd probably tell me,
"Kid, tonight
I'm sleeping in your bed."

Colors and Questions

BY BOBBI KATZ

Wouldn't it be terrible?
Wouldn't it be sad
If just one single color
Was the color that we had?
If everything was purple?
Or red? Or blue? Or green?
If yellow, pink, or orange
Was ALL that could be seen?
Can you just imagine
How the world would be
If just one SINGLE color
Was ALL we got to see?

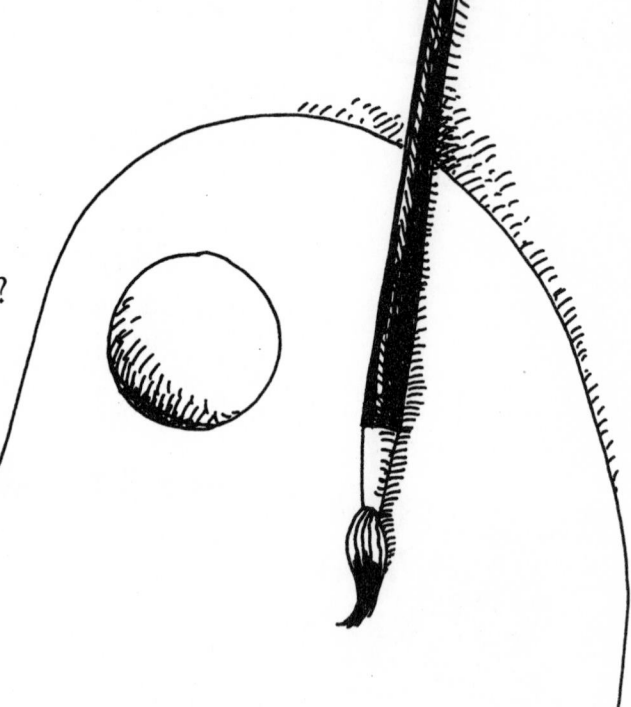
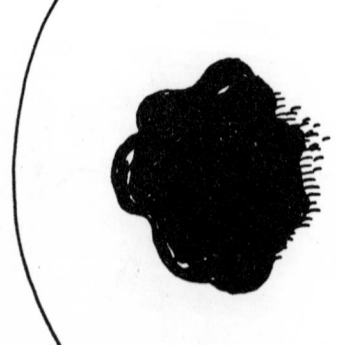

How Barney Lost His Snore

BY HELEN O'REILLY

Bears hibernate in wintertime
(you may have heard before).
There was a bear named Barney,
And he could really snore!

It bothered all his neighbors,
So they went to the store,
And chipped in for a bottle of
Some stuff called Snore-No-More!

They said, "We love you Barney, but
It's really quite a bore,
To listen to you every year—
Our ears are getting sore!"

"I didn't mean it," Barney said,
"It must have been a chore!
But now that you've all helped me out,
I won't snore anymore!"

Flu

BY TERRY COOPER

I'm wheezing
I'm sneezing

I'm coughing
   so loud.

I'm sputtering
I'm muttering
My head's in
   a cloud.

They say it's a fever,
They say it's the flu.
They say it's mysterious.
I say, "Ah . . . ah . . . CHOOO!"

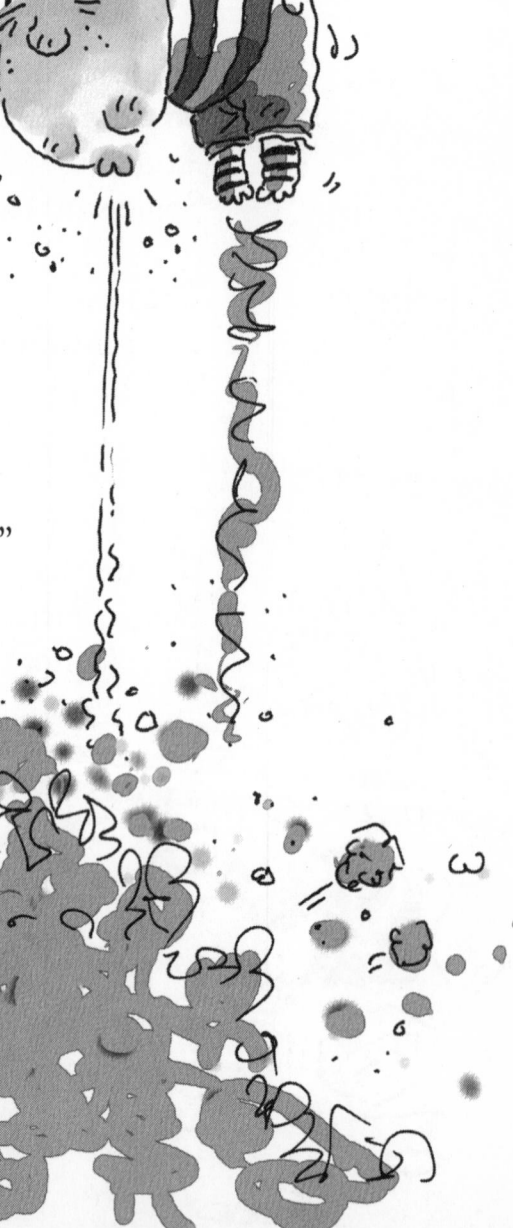

Perfect Poems With Strategies for Building Fluency: Grades 3–4   Scholastic Teaching Resources

What the Animals Said

—TRADITIONAL

"It's still dark,"
Said the lark.

"What's that?"
Said the cat.

"I want to sleep,"
Said the sheep.

"A bad habit,"
Said the rabbit.

"Of course,"
Said the horse.

"Let's have a spree,"
Said the bee.

"But where?"
Said the hare.

"In the barrow,"
Said the sparrow.

"I'm too big,"
Said the pig.

"In the house,"
Said the mouse.

But the dog said—
"Bow-wow,
It's too late now!"

Perfect Poems With Strategies for Building Fluency: Grades 3–4   Scholastic Teaching Resources

Engine, Engine

—TRADITIONAL

Engine, engine, number nine,
Ring the bell when it's time.
O-U-T spells out goes he
Into the middle of the dark blue sea.

Engine, engine, number nine,
Running on Chicago line.
When she's polished, she will shine.
Engine, engine, number nine.

Engine, engine, number nine,
Running on Chicago line.
If the train should jump the track,
Do you want your money back?

Engine, engine, number nine,
Running on Chicago line.
See it sparkle, see it shine,
Engine, engine, number nine.

Fun Is Rhyming

—TRADITIONAL

Fun is rhyming,
Huge rock climbing,
Big knot tying,
Pretend flying,
Riddle writing,
Snowball fighting,
Bike race timing,
Fun is rhyming.

Tommy Tottle

—ANONYMOUS

Young Tommy Tottle
  Had a yen
To be the best
  Of fishermen.

But what he caught—
  It's sad but true—
Was an old tin can
  And a soggy shoe.

The best of
  Fishermen, indeed!
One time he caught
  A long green weed.

And his biggest catch
  Is seldom told—
That was the time when
  He caught a cold.

Perfect Poems With Strategies for Building Fluency: Grades 3–4   Scholastic Teaching Resources

Maps

BY CAROL WESTON

Maps help us figure out
where we need to go,
which states we have visited,
and which we'd like to know.
Maps show lakes, mountains, rivers,
north, south, east, and west.
Maps show parks, beaches, cities,
But do not pick the best.
See how our nation lies
between Atlantic and Pacific?
Maps name all four oceans—
they're wonderfully specific.

A Mouse in Her Room

—TRADITIONAL

A mouse in her room woke Miss Dowd.
She was frightened
And screamed very loud.
Then a happy thought hit her,
To scare off the critter,
She sat up in bed and meowed.

Perfect Poems With Strategies for Building Fluency: Grades 3–4 Scholastic Teaching Resources

Bubble Gum

BY NINA PAYNE

I'm in trouble
made a bubble
peeled it off my nose

Felt a rock
inside my sock
got gum between my toes

Made another
told my brother
we could blow a pair

Give three cheers
now our ears
are sticking to our hair.

City Spring

BY BEVERLY MCLOUGHLAND

Spring—
Can't hold it back,
It bursts out green
From a sidewalk crack,

Like a laugh so full
You can't hold it in
With your hands held tight
Round your mouth and chin—

So full of green,
You can't hold it back,
Spring bursts out laughing
From a sidewalk crack.

I speak, I say, I talk

BY ARNOLD L. SHAPIRO

Cats purr.
Lions roar.
Owls hoot.
Bears snore.
Crickets creak.
Mice squeak.
Sheep baa.
But I SPEAK!

Monkeys chatter.
Cows moo.
Ducks quack.
Doves coo.
Pigs squeal.
Horses neigh.
Chickens cluck.
But I SAY!

Flies hum.
Dogs growl.
Bats screech.
Coyotes howl.
Frogs croak.
Parrots squawk.
Bees buzz.
But I TALK!

Trains

BY JAMES S. TIPPETT

Over the mountains,
Over the plains,
Over the rivers,
Here come the trains.

Carrying passengers,
Carrying mail,
Bringing their precious loads
In without fail.

Thousands of freight cars
All rushing on
Through day and darkness
Through dusk and dawn.

Over the mountains,
Over the plains,
Over the rivers,
Here come the trains.

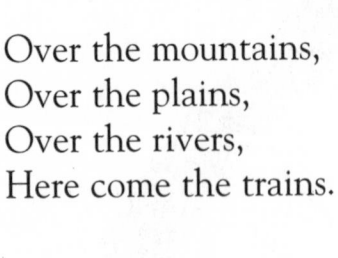

How Many Seconds in a Minute?

BY CHRISTINA G. ROSSETTI

How many seconds in a minute?
Sixty, and no more in it.

How many minutes in an hour?
Sixty for sun and shower.

How many hours in a day?
Twenty-four for work and play.

How many days in a week?
Seven both to hear and speak.

How many weeks in a month?
Four, as the swift month runn'th

How many months in a year?
Twelve the almanac makes clear.

How many years in an age?
One hundred says the sage.
How many ages in time?
No one knows the rhyme.

Laughing Time

BY WILLIAM JAY SMITH

It was laughing time
And the tall Giraffe
Lifted his head,
And began to laugh:
Ha! Ha! Ha! Ha!

And the Chimpanzee
On the gingko tree
Swung merrily down
With a Tee Hee Hee:
Hee! Hee! Hee! Hee!

"It's certainly not
Against the law!"
Croaked Justice Crow
With a loud guffaw:
Haw! Haw! Haw! Haw!

The dancing Bear
Who could never say "No"
Waltzed up and down
On the tip of his toe:
Ho! Ho! Ho! Ho!

The Donkey daintily
Took his paw,
And around they went:
Hee-Haw! Hee-Haw!
Hee-Haw! Hee-Haw!

The Moon had to smile
As it started to climb;
All over the world
It was laughing time!
Ho! Ho! Ho! Ho!
Hee-Haw! Hee-Haw!
Hee! Hee! Hee! Hee!
Ha! Ha! Ha! Ha!

Perfect Poems With Strategies for Building Fluency: Grades 3–4 Scholastic Teaching Resources

The City Mouse and the Country Mouse

BY MEISH GOLDISH

Perfect Poems With Strategies for Building Fluency: Grades 3–4   Scholastic Teaching Resources

A mouse went out to the country,
A mouse went out to the country,
A mouse went out to the country
To see his country friend.

They roamed the country plain,
Ate lots of nuts and grain.

But the mouse who went to the country
Said, "Life's too plain in the country."
He said to his friend from the country,
"Come see the city life!"

So the mice went into the city,
The mice went into the city,
The mice went into the city
To see the city life.

They ate sweet cake and cream.
The life there seemed a dream.

But the mouse new to the city
Soon was chased by a kitty.
He said, "This place may be pretty,
But I like my country home!"

And so he went back home,
And so he went back home.

Oh, the mouse who came from the country
Said, "Life is plain in the country.
It's plain but calm in the country,
So that is where I'll stay!"

Tip-Toe Tale

BY DIXIE WILSON

A fish took a notion
To come from his ocean
And take in the sights of town.
So he bought him a hat
And a coat and cravat
And a one-legged trouser of brown!
    He did!
A one-legged trouser of brown!

His suit fit so queerly
That everyone nearly
Went following out on the street!
But the best of it all
Was how handsome and tall
He could walk when he didn't have feet!
    He did!
He walked when he didn't have feet!

Now I must confess that
I surely would guess that
A fish trying walking would fail.
But with no one's advice
He walked perfectly nice
On the very tip-toes of his tail!
    He did!
On the very tip-toes of his tail!

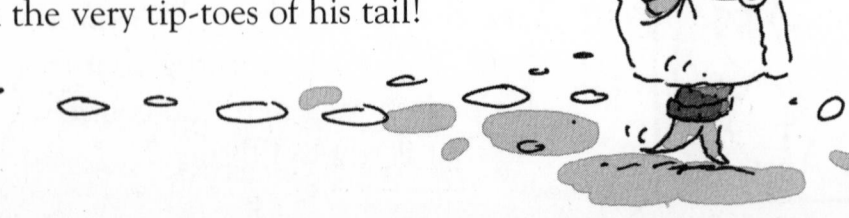

Rice Pudding

BY A. A. MILNE

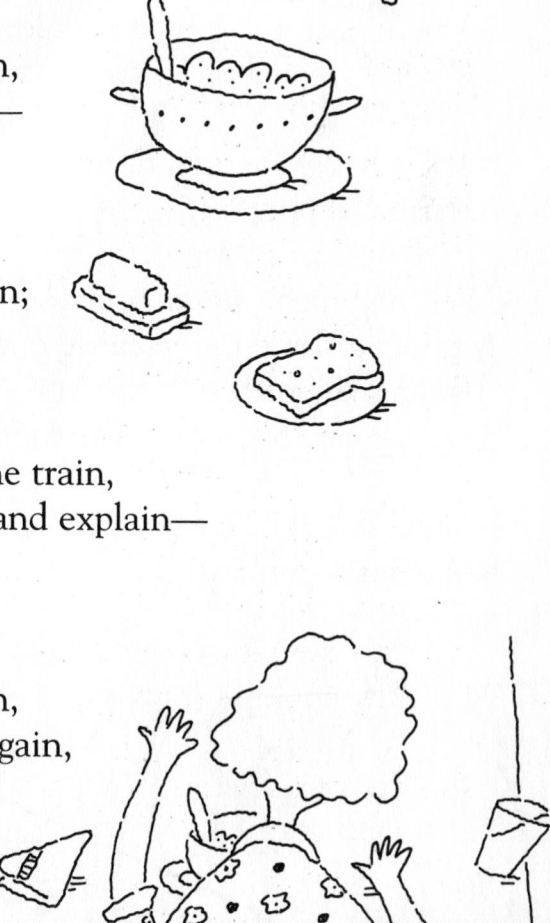

What is the matter with Mary Jane?
She is crying with all her might and main,
And she won't eat her dinner—rice pudding again—
What is the matter with Mary Jane?

What is the matter with Mary Jane?
I've promised her dolls and a daisy-chain,
And a book about animals—all in vain—
What is the matter with Mary Jane?

What is the matter with Mary Jane?
She's perfectly well, and she hasn't a pain;
What is the matter with Mary Jane?

What is the matter with Mary Jane?
I've promised her sweets and a ride in the train,
And I have begged her to stop for a bit and explain—
What is the matter with Mary Jane?

What is the matter with Mary Jane?
She's perfectly well and she hasn't a pain,
And it's lovely rice pudding for dinner again,
What is the matter with Mary Jane?

The Princess and the Pea

BY MEISH GOLDISH

Once there was a prince who tried
To find himself a perfect bride.
Yet with each princess, he couldn't decide,
For none seemed right, and he wondered:

Is she a real princess indeed?
Is she a *real* princess?

Then one night, as rain did pour,
A princess came to the castle door.
"I am a real princess," she swore.
So the queen planned a way to find out.

Is she a real princess indeed?
Is she a *real* princess?

Continued

Perfect Poems With Strategies for Building Fluency: Grades 3–4 Scholastic Teaching Resources

On a bed the queen placed a pea,
Then piled 20 mattresses carefully,
Then piled 20 quilts high as can be!
And the princess slept on top!

Is she a real princess indeed?
Is she a *real* princess?

In the morning the queen asked, "Dear,
Did you sleep well on your bed in here?"
The princess sighed, "Not well, I fear!
Something was lumpy and hard!"

The queen cried, "Son, you now can wed!
She's a real princess, as she said.
Only a real princess on top of that bed
Could feel such a tiny pea!"

She *is* a real princess indeed!
She *is* a *real* princess!

Two Little Kittens

—ANONYMOUS

Two little kittens, one stormy night,
Began to quarrel, and then to fight;
One had a mouse, the other had none,
And that's the way the quarrel begun.

"I'll have that mouse," said the biggest cat;
"You'll have that mouse? We'll see about that!"
"I *will* have that mouse," said the eldest son;
"You *shan't* have the mouse," said the little one.

I told you before 'twas a stormy night,
When these two little kittens began to fight;
The woman seized her sweeping broom,
And swept the two kittens right out of the room.

The ground was covered with frost and snow,
And the two little kittens had nowhere to go;
So they laid them down on the mat at the door,
When the old woman finished sweeping the floor.

Then they crept in, as quiet as mice,
All wet with the snow, and as cold as ice,
For they found it was better, that stormy night,
To lie down and sleep than to quarrel and fight.

Valentine's Day

BY MEISH GOLDISH

Take some paper, take some scissors,
Cut a heart, and then design.
Write a message in the middle:
"Will you be my Valentine?"

Take a doily, add some cupids,
Paste them all into a line.
Give your doily to your best friend
As a special valentine!

Take a juice can, pick some flowers,
Put them in with colored twine.
Give your present to a loved one,
And they'll be your Valentine.

Take some gumdrops and some lollies,
And some mints, eight or nine.
Make a dandy box of candy
For your sweetest Valentine!

Here's a final gift to offer,
It's a very special sign:
Give your friendship to a loved one,
To a special Valentine.

The Land of Imagination

BY HELEN H. MOORE

Oh, there is a land where llamas
Go to bed in pink pajamas

And I know how we can get there,
You and I.

It's a place where a flamingo
Might enjoy a game of bingo

It's an easy place to get to,
If you try.

If you think that somewhere there's
A land where chickens sit on chairs,

And you'd like to go there,
You don't have to fly.

If you want to see hyenas
Dancing just like ballerinas,

Give this special kind of
traveling a try . . .

You just sit there, and you think
(You don't even have to blink)
Use your mind,
And Oh!
The animals you'll see!
When you use your imagination
You'll enjoy each new creation,
Try it once—and I'm quite certain, you'll agree!

Perfect Poems With Strategies for Building Fluency: Grades 3–4   Scholastic Teaching Resources

A Mortifying Mistake

BY ANNA M. PRATT

I studied my tables over and over,
    and backward and forward, too;
But I couldn't remember six times
    nine, and I didn't know what to do,
Till sister told me to play with my doll,
    and not to bother my head,
"If you call her 'Fifty-four' for a while,
    you'll learn it by heart," she said.

So I took my favorite, Mary Ann
    (though I thought 'twas a dreadful shame
To give such a perfectly lovely child
    such a perfectly horrid name),
And I called her my dear little "Fifty-four"
    a hundred times, till I knew
The answer of six times nine as well as
    the answer of two times two.

Next day Elizabeth Wigglesworth,
    who always acts so proud,
Said "Six times nine is Fifty-two,"
    and I nearly laughed aloud!
But I wished I hadn't when teacher said,
    "Now Dorothy, tell if you can."
For I thought of my doll and—sakes alive!—
    I answered, "*Mary Ann!*"

Shy

BY MARY ANN HOBERMAN

Sometimes when I don't want to go
To visit someone I don't know,
They never stop to ask me why.
    She's shy
    They say
    She's shy
Or if we're leaving someone's house,
They say I'm quiet as a mouse
When I forget to say good-bye.
    She's shy
    They say
    She's shy
Cat's got her tongue, they always say,
She often does clam up this way,
She's silent as a stone today.
    She's shy
    They say
    She's shy
I am not shy—or if I am
I'm not a mouse or stone or clam.
I like to look and listen to
What other people say and do.
If I can't think of things to say,
Why should I say things anyway?
    I don't see why
    That makes me shy

Spaghetti! Spaghetti!

BY JACK PRELUTSKY

Spaghetti! spaghetti!
you're wonderful stuff.
I love you, spaghetti,
I can't get enough.
You're covered with sauce
and you're sprinkled with cheese,
spaghetti! spaghetti!
oh, give me some more please.

Spaghetti! spaghetti!
piled high in a mound,
you wiggle, you wriggle,
you squiggle around.
There's slurpy spaghetti
all over my plate,
spaghetti! spaghetti!
I think you are great.

Spaghetti! spaghetti!
I love you a lot,
you're slishy, you're sloshy,
delicious and hot.
I gobble you down
oh, I can't get enough,
spaghetti! spaghetti!
you're wonderful stuff.

The World of Animals

BY MEISH GOLDISH

Animals here, animals there,
Animal homes are everywhere!
High on a mountain slope so steep
Are the yak and panda, goat and sheep.
In the grasslands, flat and wide,
The zebra and giraffe abide.
In woodland forests near the water
You'll find the bear and moose and otter.
In tropical forests with lots of rain
The toucan and the sloth remain.
Out in the desert, hot and dry,
The camel and the snake go by.
In arctic regions filled with snow,
The polar bear and penguin go.
Deep in the ocean, a watery home,
The whale and shark and octopus roam.
Animals here, animals there,
Animal homes are everywhere!

Perfect Poems With Strategies for Building Fluency: Grades 3–4   Scholastic Teaching Resources

The Sad, Sad Story of the
Piggy Who Got None

BY HELEN H. MOORE

Oh, did you ever hear about
The piggy who got none?
All the other little piggies
Had their moments in the sun.

Think about it for a minute,
Think about it if you dare.
(Take your shoes off, if you have to,
count the piggies you find there.)

First of all, as you'll remember,
Was the piggy who went out,
To the market she was going,
'Cause she liked to get about.

The next piggy-wig was different,
'Cause he didn't like to roam,
He's the quiet little piggy,
He's the one who stayed at home.

Continued

Perfect Poems With Strategies for Building Fluency: Grades 3-4   Scholastic Teaching Resources

Then there was, as you'll remember,
The young piggy who got beef,
Although really, how a pig
Can eat a cow's beyond belief!

Now, skip ahead to number five—
That energetic pig,
The story tells us he ran fast,
Though he was not so big.

But let's get back to number four,
The piggy who got none . . .
While Piggy One went out the door,
To market, to have fun,
And little Piggy Two stayed home,
And Piggy Five did run,
While Piggy Three ate roasted beef,
Without a single care,
Poor Piggy Four got nothing—NONE!
I ask you, is that fair?

Perfect Poems With Strategies for Building Fluency: Grades 3–4   Scholastic Teaching Resources